CUSTOMS AND CULTURES OF THE WORLD

MY TEENAGE LIFE IN RUSSIA

CUSTOMS AND CULTURES OF THE WORLD

My Teenage Life in AUSTRALIA

My Teenage Life in BRAZIL

My Teenage Life in CHINA

My Teenage Life in EGYPT

My Teenage Life in GREECE

My Teenage Life in INDIA

My Teenage Life in JAPAN

My Teenage Life in MEXICO

My Teenage Life in NEPAL

My Teenage Life in RUSSIA

My Teenage Life in SOUTH AFRICA

Our Teenage Life in the NAVAJO NATION

CUSTOMS AND CULTURES OF THE WORLD

MY TEENAGE LIFE IN RUSSIA

By Kathryn Hulick
with Victoria Zhivova

**Series Foreword by
Kum-Kum Bhavnani**

MASON CREST

Mason Crest
450 Parkway Drive, Suite D
Broomall, PA 19008
www.masoncrest.com

© 2018 by Mason Crest, an imprint of National Highlights, Inc.

All rights reserved. No part of this publication may be reproduced or transmitted in any form or by any means, electronic or mechanical, including photocopying, recording, taping, or any information storage and retrieval system, without permission in writing from the publisher.

Printed and bound in the United States of America.

First printing
9 8 7 6 5 4 3 2 1

Series ISBN: 978-1-4222-3899-8
ISBN: 978-1-4222-3910-0
ebook ISBN: 978-1-4222-7889-5

Library of Congress Cataloging-in-Publication Data
Names: Hulick, Kathryn, author. | Zhivova, Victoria, author. Title: My teenage life in Russia / by Kathryn Hulick with Victoria Zhivova; series foreword by Kum-Kum Bhavnani.
Description: Broomall, PA : Mason Crest, 2018. | Series: Customs and cultures of the world | Includes index.
Identifiers: LCCN 2017003259| ISBN 9781422239100 (hardback) | ISBN 9781422278895 (ebook) Subjects:
    LCSH: Russia (Federation)--Social life and customs--Juvenile literature. | Russia--Social life and customs--Juvenile literature. | Teenagers--Russia (Federation)--Social life and customs--Juvenile literature.
Classification: LCC DK510.32 .H85 2018 | DDC 305.2350947086--dc23
LC record available at https://lccn.loc.gov/2017003259

Developed and Produced by Shoreline Publishing Group.
Editor: James Buckley, Jr.
Design: Tom Carling, Carling Design Inc.
Production: Sandy Gordon
www.shorelinepublishing.com

Front cover: Dreamstime.com/cloki.

QR Codes disclaimer:

You may gain access to certain third party content ("Third-Party Sites") by scanning and using the QR Codes that appear in this publication (the "QR Codes"). We do not operate or control in any respect any information, products, or services on such Third-Party Sites linked to by us via the QR Codes included in this publication, and we assume no responsibility for any materials you may access using the QR Codes. Your use of the QR Codes may be subject to terms, limitations, or restrictions set forth in the applicable terms of use or otherwise established by the owners of the Third-Party Sites. Our linking to such Third-Party Sites via the QR Codes does not imply an endorsement or sponsorship of such Third-Party Sites, or the information, products, or services offered on or through the Third-Party Sites, nor does it imply an endorsement or sponsorship of this publication by the owners of such Third-Party Sites.

RUSSIA

R0451094632

CONTENTS

Series Foreword by Kum-Kum Bhavnani, UCSB 6

MEET VICTORIA! 8	Russian Customs 32
Russia: An Introduction 10	VICTORIA'S FREE TIME 42
VICTORIA'S SCHOOL LIFE 18	Economy and Politics in Russia 44
TIME TO EAT! 20	VICTORIA'S COUNTRY 52
Russian Culture 22	The Future of Russia 54
VICTORIA'S CITIES 30	

Text-Dependent Questions 60
Research Projects 61
Find Out More 62
Series Glossary of Key Terms 63
Index/Author 64

Key Icons to Look For

Words to Understand: These words with their easy-to-understand definitions will increase the reader's understanding of the text, while building vocabulary skills.

Sidebars: This boxed material within the main text allows readers to build knowledge, gain insights, explore possibilities, and broaden their perspectives by weaving together additional information to provide realistic and holistic perspectives.

Educational Videos: Readers can view videos by scanning our QR codes, providing them with additional educational content to supplement the text. Examples include news coverage, moments in history, speeches, iconic sports moments, and much more!

Text-Dependent Questions: These questions send the reader back to the text for more careful attention to the evidence presented here.

Research Projects: Readers are pointed toward areas of further inquiry connected to each chapter. Suggestions are provided for projects that encourage deeper research and analysis.

Series Glossary of Key Terms: This back-of-the-book glossary contains terminology used throughout this series. Words found here increase the reader's ability to read and comprehend higher-level books and articles in this field.

RUSSIA

SERIES FOREWORD
Culture: Parts = Whole

Culture makes us human.

Many of us think of culture as something that belongs to a person, a group, or even a country. We talk about the food of a region as being part of its culture (tacos, pupusas, tamales, and burritos all are part of our understanding of food from Mexico, and South and Central America).

We might also talk about the clothes as being important to culture (saris in India, kimonos in Japan, hijabs or *gallibayas* in Egypt, or beaded shirts in the Navajo Nation). Imagine trying to sum up "American" culture using just examples like these! Yet culture does not just belong to a person or even a country. It is not only about food and clothes or music and art, because those things by themselves cannot tell the whole story.

Culture is also about how we live our lives. It is about our lived experiences of our societies and of all the worlds we inhabit. And in this series—Customs and Cultures of the World—you will meet young people who will share their experiences of the cultures and worlds they inhabit.

How does a teenager growing up in South Africa make sense of the history of apartheid, the 1994 democratic elections, and of what is happening now? That is as integral to our world's culture as the ancient ruins in Greece, the pyramids of Egypt, the Great Wall of China, the Himalayas above Nepal, and the Amazon rain forests in Brazil.

But these examples are not enough. Greece is also known for its financial uncertainties, Egypt is known for the uprisings in Tahrir Square, China is known for its rapid development of megacities, Australia is known for its amazing animals, and Brazil is known for the Olympics and its football [soccer] team. And there are many more examples for each nation, region, and person, and some of these examples are featured in these books. The question is: How do you, growing up in a particular country, view your own culture? What do you think of as culture? What is your lived experience of it? How do you come to understand and engage with cultures that are not familiar to you? And, perhaps most importantly, why do you/we want to do this? And how does reading about and experiencing other cultures help you understand your own?

It is perhaps a cliché to say culture forms the central core of our humanity and our dignity. If that's true, how do young adults talk about your own cultures? How do you simultaneously understand how people apparently "different" from you live their lives, and engage with their cultures? One way is to read the stories in this series. The "authors" are just like you, even though they live in different places and in different cultures. We communicated with these young writers over the Internet, which has become the greatest gathering of cultures ever. The Internet is now central to the culture of almost everyone, with young people leading the way on how to use it to expand the horizons of all of us. From those of us born in earlier generations, thank you for opening that cultural avenue!

Let me finish by saying that culture allows us to open our minds, think about worlds different from the ones we live in, and to imagine how people very different from us live their lives. This series of books is just the start of the process, but a crucial start.

I hope you enjoy them.

—Kum-Kum Bhavnani
Professor of sociology and feminist and global studies at the University of California, Santa Barbara, and an award-winning international filmmaker.

RUSSIA

MEET VICTORIA!

> I'm Victoria Zhivova from Russia. I'm 15 years old and I'm in ninth grade.

> My family is not really big. There are 8 members: mom, dad, elder sister, elder brother, two grannies, and grandpa. My dad is a urologist and my mom is a director of our family-owned private clinic. My sis works for the TV channel as a producer. I have a lot of relatives around the world, like in Israel, and in the USA. One summer, I met my cousin, my uncle, and aunt living in Los Angeles.

Editor's Note: The images in this book are not of Victoria. She chose not to include photos of herself. We respect her privacy!

To: The Reader

Subject: My Cities

Maybe it sounds weird, but my family lives in two cities: Moscow and Saint Petersburg, because my dad, who is a doctor, has clinics in Saint Petersburg and also in Moscow. In Saint P. we live in an apartment. That's very common to live there. In Moscow, we rent a house close to my dad's workplace. That house is part of a small village in a suburb. I don't really like it as much because it's pretty boring. But there are not really houses for rent in central Moscow, so we live in this village. We mostly are in Saint Petersburg, but spend summer and other times in Moscow.

It's not very common to know your neighbors in Russia. When we see them we are just saying hello and that's it. But usually I don't know their names. In Saint Petersburg, where I live is urban but in Moscow it is rural because it's not in the city center, as I said.

Moscow

Saint Petersburg

 RUSSIA

Russia: An Introduction

Thoughts of Russia often bring to mind snow, fur hats and coats, bears, and other symbols of winter. Or else you think of the world power whose leader is in the news so often.

As for the weather, it's true that Russia is situated in the far north and winters can be long, snowy, and frigid, but summers there are as green and sunny as anywhere else in the Northern Hemisphere. Russia is a

Words to Understand

autocracy a system of government in which one person has absolute power
communism a political system in which all property is publicly owned
taiga a northern forest composed mostly of evergreen trees
tsar an emperor of early Russia
tundra treeless land with permanently frozen ground
volatile marked by frequent and often large changes

The vast land of Russia spreads across part of Europe and Asia and includes a huge diversity of landforms and habitats.

huge place—the largest country in the world by area. It stretches halfway around the globe and contains the world's largest forest and deepest lake, as well as **tundra**, **taiga**, mountains, and grasslands.

A cold and very sparsely populated region called Siberia takes up most of this vast land. However, the majority of the people in Russia, including Victoria, don't live there. They live in cities such as Moscow and St. Petersburg and in towns and villages surrounding these cities. In many ways, these places are very similar to modern metropolitan centers found elsewhere in the world. However, they also reflect the unique cultural traditions and long history of Russia.

RUSSIA

From Catherine the Great to Communism

Russia has had a **volatile** history, and has alternately been both a friend and foe to European nations and to the United States. From the 16th century through the turn of the 20th century, **tsars** ruled the country. Among them were Ivan the Terrible, who turned Russia into a police state, and Catherine the Great, who established more humane laws.

In 1917, though, everything changed. Two revolutions, one after another, ended the reign of the tsars and put Vladimir Lenin into power. In a bloody culmination of Russia's frustration with its ruling class, the revolutionaries executed Tsar Nicholas II and his family. Lenin adhered

Catherine the Great married into the Russian royal family and later became the empress for more than 30 years, helping greatly expand the Russian empire.

12

Revolutionary leader Vladimir Ulyanov became known as Lenin. He used the ideals of Marxism to lead a Communist revolution that transformed Russia.

to an ideology called Marxism that is based on the ideas of the philosophers Karl Marx and Friedrich Engels. This ideology holds that society can function without class divisions or government as long as people contribute as much as they can and take only what they need. In his Communist Manifesto, Marx wrote: "In place of the old bourgeois society with its classes and class antagonisms we shall have an association in which the free development of each is the condition for the free development of all…Workers of the world unite!"

This philosophy led to the establishment of **communism** in Russia. In 1922, Russia became part of the USSR, the Union of Soviet Socialist Republics, symbolized by a red flag adorned with a crossed hammer and

RUSSIA

Under Josef Stalin, the Soviet Union became a world power, at the cost of millions of its citizens' lives.

sickle. However, communism in practice was quite different from the ideal society that Marx and Engels had imagined. In Lenin's system, the state controlled all property and determined all prices and wages. Two years later, dictator Joseph Stalin came into power. Though he transformed the USSR into a world superpower, he did so through a reign of terror that included sending millions of people to forced labor camps. His actions led to the deaths of tens of millions of his own people.

As World War II was breaking out in 1939, Winston Churchill, the prime minister of England, said, "I cannot forecast to you the action of Russia. It is a riddle wrapped in a mystery inside an enigma." He didn't know what role Russia would play during the war. In fact, World War II started with Hitler, the leader of Germany, and Stalin signing a nonaggression pact. Neither country really trusted the other, but they knew they wouldn't be able to win a war against each other and the rest of the world. However, Germany broke that agreement and invaded Russia in 1941. After that, the USSR joined the Allied powers.

After the war ended, though, tensions between the United States and the USSR grew, escalating into the Cold War, which lasted from 1948 through 1991. As the USSR promoted communism throughout the world, the United States labeled people with ties to Russia or communism as spies or worse. The USSR and the USA both raced to develop nuclear weapons and explore outer space. Russia launched *Sputnik*, the first satellite in space, in 1957. Four years later, Russian cosmonaut Yuri Gagarin became the first person in space.

The Collapse of the USSR

In 1985, a very different kind of leader came into power in the USSR. Mikhail Gorbachev sought to reform the repressive government and troubled economy. He tried to make things better through his twin policies of *perestroika* (restructuring) and *glasnost* (openness). However, his actions could not prevent the downfall of the USSR. In 1991, the Soviet Union collapsed. Many former Soviet republics became independent nations, and Russia elected its first president, Boris Yeltsin.

Democracy has replaced communism in Russia, but it hasn't been an easy transition. In fact, some consider the current leadership of Russia to be an **autocracy**. When Yeltsin resigned the presidency in 1999, prime minister Vladimir Putin became acting president. He was officially elected in 2000 and served two consecutive terms until 2008, when he was not allowed to run again. However, he kept his grip on the country by picking his own successor, Dmitry Medvedev, and getting appointed as prime minister. Just four years later, Putin ran for the presidency again, this time for a six-year term, and won easily.

Collectivism

Though Russia is no longer a communist nation, a sense of collective work for mutual gain perseveres. While a person from a Western nation might focus more on individual success, a Russian often focuses on his or her community and family. Strong social connections are essential in Russian society, especially due to political corruption. It's often necessary to "know somebody" in order to get ahead. So it's no surprise that Russians love to spend time together eating, drinking, and sharing stories.

 RUSSIA

During Putin's 16 years—and counting—as a leader of the country, Russia has worked hard to rebuild its economy, combat corruption within the government, and reclaim its status as a world superpower. Despite international concerns with some of Russia's political tactics and policies, Putin enjoys a high approval rating of 81 percent among his own people.

Russia's National Identity

Throughout these turbulent times, the Russian people have held fast to their cultural identity and traditions. Many are proud of their ability to endure hardship. Russians are also famous for their hospitality. They tend

Former KGB officer Vladimir Putin has been the face and leader of Russia for more than a decade. His leadership has been very controversial.

to be very open about their personal lives, and may ask questions that feel intrusive to visitors. Russians are also known for an indifferent attitude towards rules. Places where people typically form lines may instead become masses of people pushing their way to the front. In *CultureShock! Russia: A Survival Guide to Customs and Etiquette*, Anna Pavlovskaya writes about an experience at a Moscow park. Hundreds of people were walking dogs past signs that said "No dogs." This relaxed attitude extends to time as well. Being half an hour late is totally normal in Russia, and a friend who plans to visit for a few minutes often ends up staying for hours.

Though these stereotypical character traits may be true of many Russians, there will always be people who don't fit the mold. Like anywhere else in the world, Russia is full of people with a vast range of personalities, backgrounds, beliefs, family traditions, and values. ✸

Russian history highlights

RUSSIA

VICTORIA'S SCHOOL LIFE

To: **The Reader**

Subject: **My School**

I'm studying in middle school. I'm in the ninth grade out of 11 school grades. My school is situated in the heart of Saint Petersburg. It's a very beautiful and historic place near the Fontanka River, the Kazan Cathedral, and the Aleksandrinsky Theatre.

ORT!: My school is not typical for Russia. It's small; there are about 500 students. (In regular schools there are about 1,300.) Also my school is supported by ORT [Editor's note: The letters stand for the Russian words for Organization for the Distribution of Artisanal and Agricultural Skills.] ORT Saint Petersburg was founded by the World ORT, one of the largest worldwide international educational organizations. My school is Jewish. There are two 9th grade classes. The first one is learning Hebrew, English, and Jewish traditions. And the second class is learning English and French and we call it European class. I'm studying in the European one.

My Schedule: We study six days a week, from Monday to Saturday. My school starts at 9 am and ends at 3 or 4 pm. There are about 6 or 7 classes a day. One class lasts for 45 minutes. And all our breaks are for 15 or 25 minutes. In a year we have autumn, winter, spring, and summer breaks. Autumn, winter, and spring breaks last for a week. Summer break lasts for three months.

To: The Reader

Subject: My Music

We study in accordance to the common school program approved by the state ministry of education and some local authorities. So we don't have an opportunity to skip some subjects of the state-approved program. We can just add favorite subjects and study them after main classes. Usually I have a lot of homework and sometimes spend many hours doing it. My favorite subjects are geometry, English, and Social Studies. I took part in a national competition of English language, where I won. In my school there are a lot of extra lessons available: basketball, volleyball, our special TV channel, robotics, and the musical Jewish group, where I'm singing.

What's next? In the future I want to be a lawyer. I don't want to study and live in Russia. I want to live and study in the USA. Because I think that American education is the best in the world. And also in the USA are more opportunities than in Russia.

RUSSIA

TIME TO EAT!

New Post

Victoria Zhivova
My Favorite Foods
Like • Comment • Share

I usually eat three times a day. My breakfast consists of oatmeal or omelet and tea with milk. At school I don't like to eat so I have a bite there, with bars or some fruits. After classes I go at home and have a lunch. I prefer meat or chicken and salad. And my dinner is yogurt or fruits.

I like to taste cuisines of all over the world. My favorites are Italian—I like pizza and pasta—and Chinese, because I like how they mix products. Me and my friends also go to some fast food places. We like hamburgers, chicken nuggets, and French fries. Also sometimes we are going to restaurants; it's normal to see teenagers in restaurants. When I have free time I like to cook. I can cook pasta with tomatoes and cake with apples!

20

RUSSIAN DISHES

In Russian cuisine there are a lot of traditional dishes: *pelmeni* (it looks like Italian ravioli with meat); *borscht* (it's like a meat soup with beets, carrots, and potatoes); *olivier* or Russian salad made of potatoes, carrots, pickled cucumbers, and green peas; *shchi* (also kind of a meat soup with cabbage); and *venigred* (potato, carrots and beet salad with sunflower oil dressing).

RUSSIA

Russian Culture

Russian culture encompasses everything from food and drink to art, music, literature, sports, and more. Though many contemporary Russians regularly enjoy foods and entertainment from other countries and cultures around the world, they continue to embrace their own traditions as well. Russia is especially well known for its contributions to literature, classical music, ballet, architecture, painting, and science.

Welcoming Guests

The first thing visitors to Russia notice is usually the food. Hospitality is of utmost importance in Russia, and being a good host or hostess means providing ample food and drink to guests. Pavlovskaya writes: "According to Russian traditions, if guests come round, your table should be so covered with food that after everybody has eaten their fill, there is still food left over." Sometimes a visit is planned ahead of time, but often guests arrive unexpectedly, and that is not considered rude. No matter whether

Words to Understand

caviar   pickled fish eggs

censorship   the practice of controlling media to remove unwanted material

propaganda   information that promotes a specific viewpoint

vodka   an alcoholic beverage that originated in Russia

Caviar is a Russian delicacy. The tiny, salty pods are actually the eggs of a fish called the sturgeon that lives in icy rivers in Russia.

a visit is planned or spontaneous, whether it's a regular mealtime or ten o'clock at night, a Russian host must always offer food and drink, and it's offensive for the guest not to partake. At the very least, the guest must eat some bread, even if he or she only stopped by for a moment.

A full meal with guests usually begins with several different kinds of cold salads and other appetizers ranging from cheese and salted mushrooms to fish delicacies including **caviar**. Bread is always on the table as well. The soup course is next. Borscht is a popular Russian soup made with beets and cabbage. However, a meat and cabbage soup called *shchi* is more traditional. After all this comes the main dish, which may be chicken, beef, pork, or *pelmeni*, a meat-stuffed pasta similar in size and shape to Italian tortellini. Finally, everyone drinks tea and has dessert, which may be cookies, cakes, or biscuits with jam and honey. The meal may last hours,

RUSSIA

The samovar is the traditional way to serve tea in Russia.

and often includes rounds of alcoholic drinks, typically **vodka**. Guests almost always bring gifts when they visit, often good-quality tea, cookies, sweets for any children, flowers, or alcoholic beverages. The gesture of bringing a gift is more important than the item.

Food and Drink

Russians typically eat a large breakfast, and then have their main meal at lunchtime. Often, students or even business people will go home to eat lunch. Dinner is usually a smaller meal. In traditional Russian cuisine, spices are not common. Most Russian dishes consist of meat that has been fried, boiled, braised, or baked for a long time. Bread is a staple food in the Russian diet, and in villages, many families still bake their own. Another traditional food is bliny, or pancakes. These may be served with savory toppings as an appetizer, or with jam, cream, or condensed milk for dessert. While it's traditional for Russians to eat at home, they do visit restaurants occasionally. In big cities, a variety of options is available, ranging from McDonald's and Kentucky Fried Chicken to Japanese and Italian restaurants.

When it comes to drinks, tea is served with nearly every meal, though some Russians do drink coffee in the morning. The traditional device for boiling water for tea is called a samovar. Russians also enjoy seltzer water and soft drinks. A traditional drink called *kvass* is basically liquefied bread. It's sort of like a sweet, non-alcoholic beer. However, Russians are most famous for drinking lots of vodka. As the drink flows after a meal, everyone starts making toasts and singing songs together.

The prevalence of vodka has its downside. An estimated one out of five Russian men die from alcohol-related causes, according to a report from the World Health Organization. Despite the efforts of several Russian leaders, including Lenin and Gorbachev, to tackle the problem of alcoholism, it continues to plague the country. The root of the alcohol issue seems to be that drinking shots of vodka or other alcoholic beverages goes hand in hand with hospitality. It's a gesture of friendship and solidarity to drink together. A common Russian toast goes: "May we always have a reason for a party!"

Art, Music, and Literature

Many great painters, writers, composers, and other artists have called Russia home. Most early Russian art was religious in nature and tied to the Russian Orthodox Church, a Christian faith that has been the dominant religious entity in Russia since the 10th century. The "onion dome" style of architecture so closely associated with Russia originated on Orthodox churches. Russia also became famous for its religious icons. These are depictions of religious figures, typically small in

One theory of the origin of onion domes is that they let snow slide off easily.

25

RUSSIA

Ballet has long been a favorite of Russian audiences, and some of the most famous dancers in history have come from Russia.

size and painted on wood. Icons are displayed in churches, used in ceremonies, or kept in the home.

Russia is also known for its contributions to classical music, ballet, opera, and theater. By the mid-19th century, Russia had become the center of the dance world. One of the world's most beloved ballets, *The Nutcracker*, was first produced in Moscow's Imperial Theaters for Christmas 1892. Famous Russian composer Pyotr Ilyich Tchaikovsky wrote the music. Among Tchaikovsky's other well-known works are his symphonies, the ballet *Swan Lake*, and a set of pieces for piano titled *The Seasons*. Other famous Russian composers include Sergei Rachmaninoff and Dmitri Shostakovich.

Literature is another area of Russian culture with a strong history. Russians especially revere the 19th century poet Alexander Pushkin. He is considered the father of Russian literature, and is known for his love poems. Other famous writers include Nikolai Gogol, author of the short story *The Nose*; Anton Chekhov, a famous playwright; Fyodor Dostoyevsky, who wrote *Crime and Punishment*; and Leo Tolstoy, author of *War and Peace*. Russians have also made their mark on fine art. Natal'ia Sergeevna Goncharova developed costume and stage designs for the ballet. Vasiliy Kandinsky was a famous abstract artist, and painter Marc Chagall developed a unique form of his art.

All Russian artists have had to contend with **censorship** in one form or another. Even during the time of the tsars, newspapers and books often had to be approved by a censorship committee. During the Soviet era, the government tightened its control over many different forms of art and produced **propaganda**. Some artists' work was banned, including a film about the Russian revolution by Sergei Eisenstein. Since the communist ideology promotes atheism, religion also came under attack. Many Russian Orthodox churches were closed. Even today, journalism, theater, television, and other forms of media face censorship.

From Science to Sports and Games

While religion was oppressed during the Soviet era, science and sports were both encouraged. Throughout the country's history, scholars have helped advance the fields of science, mathematics, and technology. Mikhail Lomonosov, one of the first great Russian scientists,

Fyodor Dostoevsky is the most famous Russian writer of all time.

RUSSIA

helped establish the Moscow State University. Ivan Pavlov, a psychologist and physician, developed the theory of classical conditioning based on experiments in which he trained dogs to drool when a bell rang. Chemist Dmitri Mendeleev created the periodic table of the elements, and rocket scientist Sergei Korolov headed the Soviet space program, which launched the first satellite and put the first man into space.

Sports and games are extremely popular in Russia. People especially enjoy watching soccer, which they call football, and ice hockey. Russia was proud to host the 2014 Olympics in Sochi. During the Soviet era, athletes' achievements were widely celebrated and fed into a sense of national pride. The ice hockey team in particular gained international fame for winning numerous world championships and Olympic gold medals. Soviet athletes also made their mark in gymnastics, track-and-field, weightlifting,

The 2014 Winter Olympics in Sochi were a chance for Russia to welcome the world to its land and show that it could handle a major event.

Learn Russian

The Russian language uses the Cyrillic alphabet. This is especially confusing for English speakers because many of the letters look the same but sound different. For example, the Russian letter "B" is pronounced "V," "H" is really "N" and "P" sounds like "R." The Russian language also does not include words for "the" or "a." Believe it or not, those articles aren't really necessary for communication. Want to speak some Russian? Here are some phrases to get you started.

Hi	Privet (PREE-vyet)	привет
My name is ___	Menya zovut ___ (men-YA za-VOOT)	Меня зовут ___
Please	Pozhaluysta (pa-ZHA-loo-sta)	пожалуйста
Thank you	Spasibo (spa-SEE-ba)	спасибо
How are you?	Kak dela (KAK de-LA)	Как дела?
Yes / No	Da (da) / Net (nyet)	да / нет
I don't know	Ya ne znayu (ya nee ZNA-yoo)	Я не знаю
Happy birthday	S dnyem rozhdeniya (sdnyem rozh-DEN-ee-ya)	С днём рождения!

wrestling, and boxing, and Russian competitors continue to dominate in these sports today. However, recently Russian athletes have been shown to have used performance-enhancing drugs. Its entire track team was banned from the 2016 Olympics in Brazil. This practice, a holdover from the Soviet system, continues to plague Russian international sports.

Russia also leads the world in competitive chess. Since 1948, numerous Russian men and women have become grand masters or claimed the title of world champion in chess. Finally, the popular video game Tetris was developed in Russia during the Cold War. ✸

RUSSIA

VICTORIA'S CITIES

To: The Reader

Subject: My Cities

I'm happy to live in both biggest and most famous cities of Russia: St. Petersburg and Moscow. I invite teenagers and their families from all over the world to come and visit the nicest cities of Russia, St. Petersburg and Moscow. Here's a look at both of them!

St. Petersburg: I think that Saint Petersburg is the most beautiful city. So when my friends from other countries ask me which city I recommend them to visit first I always say: "Saint Petersburg!" It's the cultural heart of Russia. People call it "Northern Venice" because there are a lot of rivers and channels and the architecture really looks like the best places of classic European. From 1703 to 1917, St. Petersburg was the capital of the Russian Empire. There are a lot of museums, churches, cathedrals and historical buildings. The real beauties of St. Petersburg's places of interest are Peter and Paul fortress, St. Isaacs Cathedral, the Admiralty, Kazansky Cathedral, the Church of the Savoir on the Blood. There is also beautiful Vasilievsky Island with its monumental stock exchange building and old-fashioned gas-lamp-lit houses.

My favorite museum is Hermitage. It's the museum of art and culture. Hermitage is one of the largest and oldest museums in the world. It was founded in 1764. And also I like Peterhof Palace. It's the place where my soul relaxes. Peterhof is a series of palaces, gardens, and fountains located in a beautiful suburb. It can be reached in summer by fast boat. I do recommend visiting it in summer, though!

To: The Reader
Subject: Moscow

Moscow is now the capital of Russia and it's one of the oldest cities in my country, founded in 1197 by the Duke Yuryi Dolgorukiy. In Moscow one can enjoy the Kremlin or Red Square, of course. But I like to see the Russian art at the Tretyakovskaya Gallery. I used to visit that museum when I was younger. The program for elementary school children is beautiful in this museum. They taught us a history of Russian art, conducted thematic excursions, and explained how artists created their paintings. Another famous museum of Moscow is Pushkin's Museum of Art. It's more devoted to western art pretty much like the Hermitage in St. Petersburg, but a lot smaller.

 RUSSIA

Russian Customs

Customs and traditions in Russia stem from a number of different roots. First of all, Russia's very early history of paganism still shows itself in common **superstitions**, fairy tales, and some rural traditions. Many of the holidays celebrated in Russia, though, mark religious occasions observed by the Russian Orthodox Church. Finally, communist ideology of the Soviet era asserted an influence as well, and left behind numerous **secular** holidays. Of course, all holidays in Russia involve lots of food, drink, and celebration. The most exciting time of the year in Russia is the New Year's season.

Calendar Confusion

Like other Christians, members of the Russian Orthodox Church celebrate Easter and Christmas. However, the dates when they celebrate these holidays don't match up with most of the rest of the world. Orthodox Christians

---

Words to Understand

equinox a date that occurs twice each year when day and night are the same length

secular not religious

superstition a belief based on no reason or knowledge that places special significance on a specific thing or action

During part of the Orthodox Easter service, a priest uses a whip-like brush to sprinkle holy water on the faithful.

celebrate the Christmas holidays on January 6 and 7. These are actually the original dates that the Roman Empire designated as Christmas Eve and Christmas Day way back in 325. But when Europe switched over to a new date system in 1582, the Pope moved Christmas Eve to December 24 and Christmas to December 25 to fit the new calendar.

RUSSIA

Most Eastern Orthodox Christians in Russia and elsewhere continued to observe holidays according to the old Julian calendar. In fact, all of Russia kept the Julian calendar until the revolution in 1917. The date for Easter is determined based on the first full moon after the **equinox**. While the date of the equinox is different on the two calendars, full moons are the same no matter what calendar you follow. So some years Orthodox Easter and Western Easter fall on the same day. Orthodox Christians also observe Old New Year's Day two weeks later, on what the rest of the world says is January 14. Of course, Russians love to celebrate. So some make up for all this date confusion by celebrating the holidays twice!

Happy New Year!

Many of the customs and traditions that people in Western nations associate with Christmas happen during New Year's celebrations in Russia on December 31 and January 1. After the 1917 revolution, the communist regime banned Christmas and all other religious celebrations. But many of these traditions simply migrated to New Year's instead. Instead of a Christmas tree, Russians put up a New Year's tree, which is often small and plastic. However, they also decorate with lots of lights and ornaments. The Russian Santa Claus, "Dyed Moroz" (Father Frost), brings gifts to children for New Year's. He rides in a sledge drawn by horses, accompanied by his granddaughter, "Snegurochka" (Snow Maiden).

On New Year's Eve, Russian families tend to celebrate at home until midnight with lots of food. Traditional New Year's foods include champagne, caviar, mandarin oranges, and salads. The most essential New Year's salad is called *olivier*. It's a hearty mixture of potatoes, peas, carrots, pickles, hard-boiled eggs, and mayonnaise. At midnight on New Year's, the president speaks on TV about his wishes for the coming year. Then Russians take to the streets and watch extravagant firework shows. Many people set off their own fireworks and sparklers. The partying continues long into the night.

Russians celebrate a number of **secular** holidays, partly thanks to the anti-religious stance of the Soviet government. Examples include Defender of the Motherland Day on February 23, which was originally a day to celebrate the Soviet Army, but has become a celebration of all men. On March 8, Russians celebrate International Women's Day by giving gifts

During the Christmas holidays, colorful lights and deocrations are raised outside the famous Bolshoi Theater in Moscow.

RUSSIA

The Russian Victory Day parade on May 9 has a military feel, with soldiers and others marching to commemorate the end of World War II.

to all women and girls in their lives. Victory Day on May 9 marks the date when Germany surrendered to the USSR in World War II. Cosmonautics Day on April 12 commemorates when Russian Yuri Gagarin became the first man in space.

Family Celebrations

Russian people love any excuse to throw a party. Birthdays are often celebrated several times, for example once with family and friends and another time at work. These celebrations, though, must fall on or after the actual date of the birthday—it's bad luck to celebrate beforehand. Other events, such as getting a promotion at work, retiring, or even buying a new car or house, are often marked with small parties including the usual spread of food and drink. According to superstition, failing to celebrate an event means that it will not bring success.

It should come as no surprise, then, that weddings are an extravagant occasion. In many ways, a Russian wedding resembles a wedding in the United States. The bride usually wears a white dress and veil, the groom wears a suit, and the couple exchanges rings. The actual marriage

A Russian bride and groom meet at an official government office to formalize their wedding. A church ceremony might follow with family and friends.

37

RUSSIA

usually takes place at a registry office, though having a religious ceremony at a church is becoming more popular. Afterwards, the couple visits an historical place, such as the Kremlin in Moscow, to pay their respects and take pictures. Finally, everyone attends a banquet at a restaurant or other venue. Families go to great lengths to throw a wedding celebration as large and opulent as possible. The bigger the wedding, many believe, the longer the couple will stay together. Russian wedding traditions include showering the couple with seeds, stealing the bride's shoe, and presenting the couple bread and salt. The bride and groom break off pieces of the bread, dip it in the salt, and feed it to each other.

During the Russian Orthodox marriage service, attendants hold crowns over the heads of the couple, symbolizing that the couple are king and queen of their home.

Many Russian dachas are designed to look like older, more traditional homes. The heavy logs cover insulation that makes the inside of the homes cozy.

Funeral banquets are also a part of Russian tradition. A large feast is served on the day of the funeral, and smaller banquets are held on the ninth and fortieth day after the death. These traditions likely date back to pagan times. Just as for a wedding, the family invites as many people as possible to the funeral. The table is full of food and drink, with one spot left empty for the person who passed away.

When families go on vacation in Russia, it's traditional to visit a house in the country, called a *dacha*. While at the dacha, Russians typically enjoy playing sports, fishing, gardening, picking mushrooms, and visiting the *banya*, a type of sauna or steam bath.

RUSSIA

Social Conventions

Despite the joyous times Russians share together, they don't smile a lot, even for photos. It's considered strange and foolish to smile at strangers. In *CultureShock!* Anna Pavlovskaya describes how employees at the first McDonald's in Russia were told to smile at customers. "People think that we're complete idiots," the employees said. Despite Russian's stony faces, they tend to dress up much more than Americans do. Women wear makeup and high heels regularly, and men wear ironed shirts and pants.

The Matryoshka, or nesting doll, is a well-known symbol of Russia. Originally intended for children, the toy became wildly popular around the world in the early 20th century.

Many Russian social customs are very conservative and traditional. Though women in Russia have equal rights as men under the law, it is typical for the husband to lead the family as head of the household. And though many Russian women pursue careers, they also take on the majority of household duties such as cooking, cleaning, and caring for children. Women are prohibited from entering more than 450 jobs deemed too difficult or dangerous, such as firefighter, blacksmith, or train driver. Gay rights are not widely supported in Russia, and openly gay people there face discrimination.

Marriage and family are central to Russian life. Independence is not valued very highly in this country—rather, people expect and approve of dependence on each other. An unmarried person, especially an unmarried woman, may become a social outcast, so Russian women often get married in their early 20s. Large Russian families often live in close quarters in small apartments or houses. It's common for young families to live with either the husband or wife's parents. ✽

Russian Superstitions

As in many other countries, black cats and broken mirrors are associated with bad luck in Russia. But some other Russian superstitions are more surprising.

- When announcing good news, you should spit three times over the left shoulder (or pretend to spit). This ensures that the good thing actually happens and isn't ruined.
- Never whistle indoors. This will lead to financial problems in the future.
- Doorways are bad news. Handing things through a doorway or holding a conversation over a doorway invites misfortune.
- Always give an odd number of flowers. Even numbers are only for funerals.
- People, especially young women, should not sit directly on the ground or any cold surface, or they may not be able to have children.
- Gifts for a baby should be bought only after it is born. Similarly, birthdays should only be mentioned or celebrated on or after the actual birthday.
- Before a big trip, everyone in the family should sit together in silence for a moment. This helps ensure a safe journey.

RUSSIA

VICTORIA'S FREE TIME

To: The Reader

Subject: My Free Time

I have a lot of hobbies. I'm going to musical school and I play piano there. My favorite composer is Vivaldi. Also, I'm going to the drama studio. This drama studio consists of three parts: drama, singing, and dancing. At the end it looks like a musical. Also I'm going to the swimming pool. Some years ago I used to do synchronized swimming.

I'm going to musical school and I play piano there. My favorite composer is Vivaldi.

ROMEO AND JULIET!

To: The Reader

Subject: My Free Time

With my friends, I like to visit movie premieres. Also, my family and I go to the theatre every month. I like symphony concerts, too. I like ballets more than operas. My favorite ballet is *Romeo and Juliet*.

I do love Moscow drama theaters where one can see very interesting productions of modern and classic Russian and foreign authors. My family prefers to visit drama theaters in Moscow rather than in St. Petersburg.

43

RUSSIA

Economy and Politics in Russia

Since communism in Russia ended with the fall of the Soviet Union in 1991, the country has gone through decades of political and economic turmoil. As the first president of Russia, Boris Yeltsin, moved businesses and property from governmental to private control, a group of **oligarchs** emerged. These incredibly wealthy, powerful people controlled most of Russia's energy, media, and other industries, while poverty plagued average Russians. When Vladimir Putin took office in 2000, the population of Russia was decreasing. People weren't having very many children and many were dying young. Putin took a more **authoritarian** stance and restored governmental control of many industries.

Words to Understand

authoritarian a system that favors obedience to an authority over individual freedom

nationalism patriotism marked with a sense of superiority over other countries

natural gas a flammable gas composed mainly of methane and used as fuel

oligarch one of a small group of people who have control over a country

sanction a penalty for disobeying a rule

Though not everyone can afford to shop at such places, Moscow does have many large shopping malls. The largest is here at Afimall.

By 2010, the population had started growing again. Between 1999 and 2006, disposable income doubled in the country. Though Russia has become more prosperous, the gap between extreme wealth and extreme poverty remains stark. Moscow is ranked third after New York and Beijing on a list of cities with the most billionaires. An abundance of flashy advertising in Russia's biggest cities promotes consumerism, and those who have wealth tend to flaunt it. However, Moscow is also home to an estimated 100,000 homeless people. In addition, people living in the countryside often don't have running water or reliable electricity.

45

RUSSIA

Russia's economic prosperity is most closely tied to one thing: energy. Oil and petroleum products, **natural gas**, and coal are Russia's biggest exports. In fact, 70 percent of Russia's export income comes from oil and gas, according to the British Broadcasting Corporation.

Russia's massive oil reserves have made the industry the economic leader in the country, but any drop in prices has a long domino effect on the nation.

An Energy Economy

In 2013, Russia led the world in oil production and was the second-largest producer of dry natural gas, according to the U.S. Energy Information Association. These resources mainly come from West Siberia, a frigid region stretching from the border with Kazakhstan to the Arctic Ocean. Of all the countries in the world, Russia has the largest reserves of natural gas. This resource has grown in importance for several reasons, including the development of hydraulic fracturing ("fracking") technology and the fact that natural gas seems less likely to worsen climate change or pollution compared to oil and coal. However, Russia continues to increase its oil production as well, and recently began drilling offshore for oil in the Arctic.

In addition to a huge quantity of "black gold," or oil, the vast, frozen expanse of Siberia yields real gold as well. During the early 19th century, Russia was the world's leading gold producer, and it remains a leader in the world gold market today. The freezing tundra had yet another secret hidden away: diamonds. After diamonds were discovered in Siberia in the 1950s, Russia has become the world's leading diamond producer by volume.

Rising global prices for oil spurred Russia's economic boom during the 2000s. However, since 2014, oil prices have dropped. Paired with international **sanctions** on the country, this has resulted in an economic recession. Some experts warn that Russia's economy is too dependent on its raw material exports, which also include aluminum and iron.

In addition to energy and raw material mining, other important industries in Russia include manufacturing of aircraft and space vehicles, defense equipment, transportation equipment, communications equipment, agricultural machinery, medical and scientific instruments, and consumer products. However, more than half of Russians work in service industries, such as the government, education, retail, or tourism. Though

RUSSIA

unemployment is low in Russia, this does not mean that the labor market is strong. In response to economic difficulty, Russian employers tend to pay lower salaries, shorten the workweek, or send employees on unpaid leave.

In Russia, it is common to curry favor with superiors or officials through family connections or bribes. In fact, it's often nearly impossible to accomplish anything without some sort of personal connection or bribery. This corruption is so integrated into Russian life that people accept it as the normal way to do business.

Putin's Autocracy

Strong, powerful leaders such as Putin are a part of Russian identity. A poll revealed that 75 percent of Russians said that a strong economy was better for the country than a good democracy. Though Russia is currently a democracy by name, its history is autocratic (a system of government in which one person has absolute power). Many consider President Vladimir Putin's hold over Russia to be an autocracy as well. He has ruled Russia in one way or another for more than 16 years, and his political party, United Russia, is almost entirely unopposed in elections. It also controls a huge majority of seats in the State Duma, the Russian legislature. In addition, the government asserts control over the media, making it difficult for opposition parties to get their message out. It's also very hard to organize protests or rallies that run counter to the current government.

As Russia's economy boomed during the late 2000s and early 2010s, the country began to assert itself more in world politics. The conflict in Ukraine has been one of the most troubling aspects of Russia's recent history. Since revolutionaries in Ukraine overthrew that country's government in 2014, the country has been fighting with Russia over control of a region called Crimea. Many Ukrainians favor alignment with the European Union—they want to be free from the influence of the former

Russian troops moved into the Crimea, an area of neighboring Ukraine, and claimed it, over the objections of the international community.

Soviet Union. But Russia prefers to maintain some control over this former territory, and some suspect that Russia has been arming separatists in the Ukraine who wish to align with Russia. In 2014, a Malaysia Airlines passenger plane was shot down as it flew over the Ukraine, allegedly by these separatists.

RUSSIA

The giant of Russia's energy industry is a company called Gazprom, which is mostly owned by the Russian government and largely controlled by Putin. He keeps energy prices low in Russia, and wields Gazprom's influence as a weapon in foreign policy. For example, he has cut off access to gas in Ukraine during the ongoing conflict there. In addition to the conflict in the Ukraine, Russia has dealt with ongoing conflicts in Chechnya, an area dominated by radical Islamists.

In response to Russia's actions in Ukraine, the European Union and United States imposed a number of sanctions. These include bans on exports to Russia of equipment for military use, bans on exports of oil industry technology, and travel bans on some officials and leaders. Russian state banks are also not allowed to get long-term loans in the EU.

These sanctions seem only to have hardened Russia's sense of **nationalism**. Putin's Russia emphasizes conservative values and a strong, central government. Russia has been reluctant to align its interests with Western nations and integrate into the world economy. Instead, many Russians take pride in the strength and independence of their country and power of their leader. ✽

Music Protest

Not everyone is Russia agrees with Putin's ideas and vision for Russia. A rock group has gained international notoriety for its colorful and creative acts of protest against Putin. The band's performances have even led to the arrest of its members, under the criminal charge of "hooliganism." In an interview with *Vice*, Serafima, one of the band's anonymous members, said, "We realized that this country needs a militant, punk-feminist, street band that will rip through Moscow's streets and squares... and enrich the Russian cultural and political opposition with themes that are important to us; gender and LGBT rights... and the domination of males in all areas of public discourse."

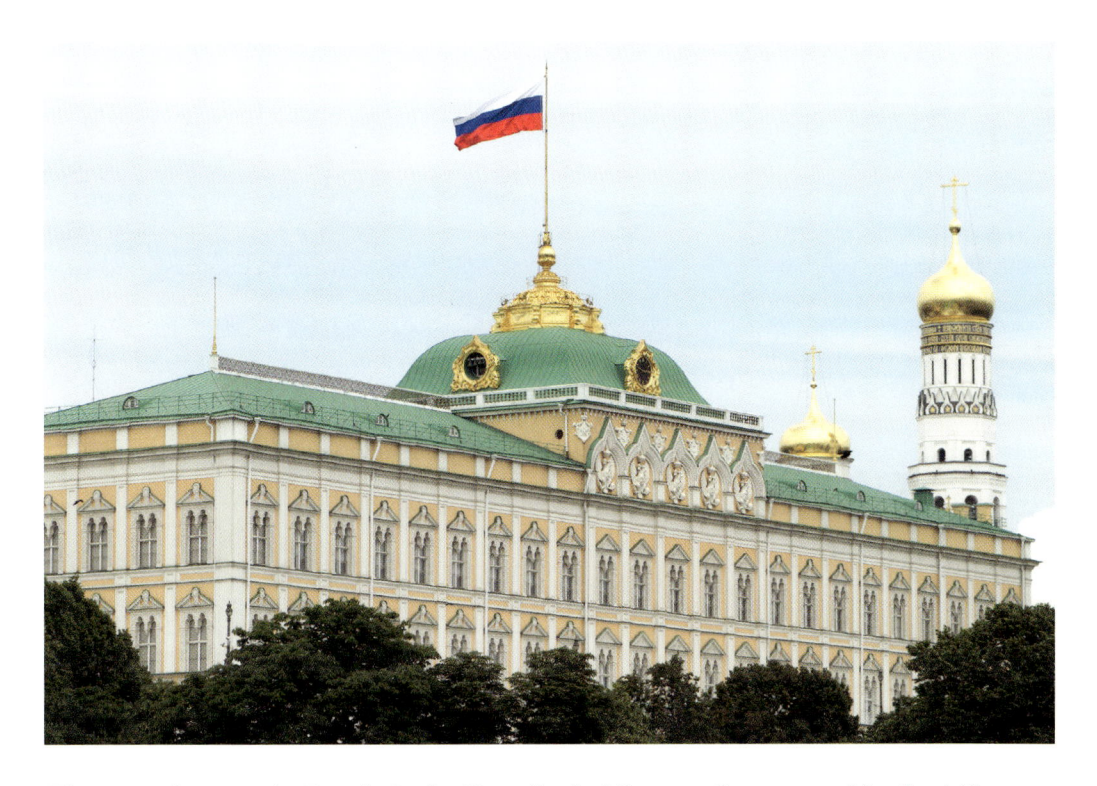

The seat of power in Russia is the Kremlin in Moscow. Constructed in the 14th century, the fortress includes four palaces and four cathedrals enclosed within a wall adorned with towers. The tsars and Soviet leaders ruled from the Kremlin. Now, it is the official residence of the president.

Inside Russia's economy

51

RUSSIA

Victoria's Country

I LOVE MY HOMELAND

Russia is my homeland. Russia is rich in picturesque forests, vast fields, deep lakes, rivers and seas. In Russia there are a lot of beautiful places, where you can relax.

Chuvash

Tatar

Russia is a multi-ethnic country with a peace-loving, kind, sympathetic people. Many people inhabit different parts of Russia: Russian, Tatar, Bashkir, Chuvash, Karelia, Uzbeks and others.

Bashkir

Uzbek

53

RUSSIA

The Future of Russia

Ever since the decade of political and economic turmoil that Russians endured after the fall of the Soviet Union, the country has been moving back towards a more conservative, authoritarian government. There is every reason to expect that in the near future, Putin will continue to wield power and pursue his isolationist vision for Russia. At the same time, many young, urban people in Russia are becoming increasingly liberal and voicing frustration with corruption and discrimination in their society. While the number of these **dissidents** remains small, there is a chance that they could change the direction of their country.

Words to Understand

blacklist   to ban or prevent from being seen or heard

dissident   in an authoritarian state, a person who disagrees strongly with a government's policies and works actively to change them

exile   a state of being removed from one's native country

fragmentation   breaking up into smaller parts

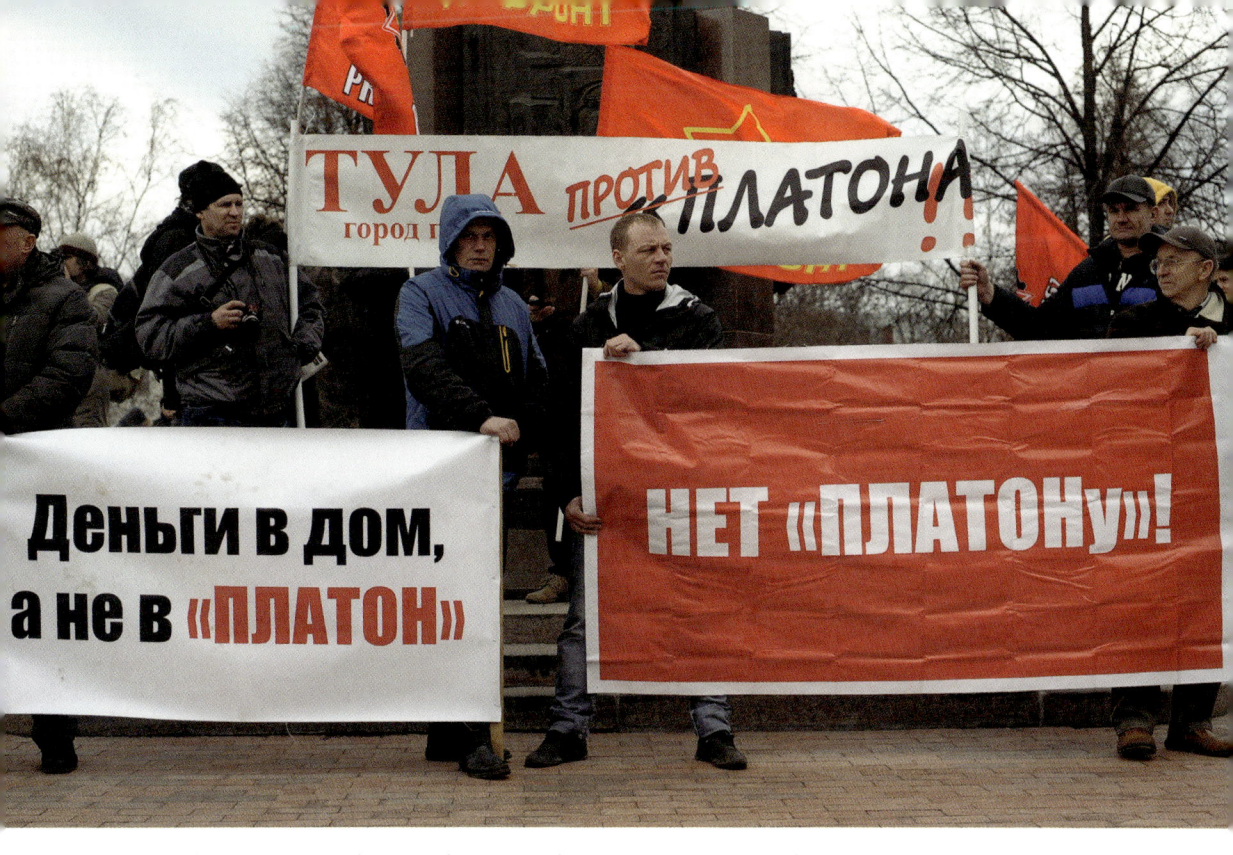

Many labor groups in Russia are unhappy. Here, truck drivers in Moscow protest against a proposed new tax on their work.

Hardship Ahead

Many analysts agree that Russia is in for a rough future, especially if oil prices continue to stay low. The country will likely have to develop new industries, introduce economic reforms, and lower or even eliminate its dependence on income from oil exports. In addition, Russia may lose power and influence as its population declines and former republics join forces with each other to oppose Russian policies. A 2015 report from the firm Strategic Forecasting predicts trouble for Russia: "We expect Moscow's authority to weaken substantially, leading to the formal and informal **fragmentation** of Russia." A World Bank study of Russia also found that the Russian economy is weakening thanks to an aging population, unproductive workers, and the lack of investment in businesses.

RUSSIA

Though he became a rich man in the new Russia, Mikhail Khodorkovsky was forced to leave when he objected to government programs.

In addition, freedoms will likely continue to diminish in Russia. Putin's government has been asserting more and more control over the country, including censorship of television, the Internet, and other media. The government regularly **blacklists** websites and has put people in prison for posting or sharing material that contradicts its views. However, Russians are used to hardship. Some take pride in their ability to sacrifice and suffer for the greater good. Many are of the opinion that only a strong, authoritarian government can keep order and ensure predictability, which is more important than freedom.

Though Putin enjoys strong support among Russians, some do oppose him. Mikhail Khodorkovsky is the leader of the opposition party Open Russia. A former businessman who accumulated incredible wealth during the 1990s, Khodorkovsky spent time in prison after being convicted of fraud in 2005. Many suspected that the conviction was politically motivated. Now in **exile** in Switzerland, Khodorkovsky regularly speaks out against Putin. In an opinion piece for *Vice* news, he wrote: "The monopolization of the economy, the destruction of freedoms and civil liberties, the liquidation of democratic institutions—all of this has given Putin immense power, but it has spelled disaster for the economy." Khodorkovsky believes that another future is possible for Russia: one in which the country becomes economically dynamic and acts as a reliable partner on the world stage rather than as a bully.

The past and the future: A young Russian girl and her mother look at space gear from Russia's long history of exploration.

RUSSIA

A Friend in Donald Trump?

After Russia claimed Crimea as its territory, the relationship between the US and Russia soured. But then Donald Trump won the 2016 US presidential election. It was no secret that Putin wanted Trump to win. In fact, US intelligence discovered that the Russian government had stolen and leaked information likely intended to interfere with the election process. Putin was also one of the first world leaders to congratulate Trump on his victory. Trump's vision for the US includes much less involvement in world affairs, a situation that would mean less opposition against Putin. In addition, Trump has said that he would look into recognizing Crimea as part of Russia rather than the Ukraine, a stance that goes against the views of almost every other leader in the US and Europe. With the United States as an ally, Russia would be in a less hazardous position in political and economic negotiations. This is a developing situation, to be sure.

However, many Russians don't see Putin's actions as those of a bully. They see their leader as a strong person who stands up for his country. Giving in to outside demands would make Russia look weak, they feel.

Searching for a New National Identity

In many ways, Russia is a young nation still forming a national identity for itself. In the 18th and 19th centuries, Orthodox Christianity provided a moral structure. Then the revolutions of 1917 replaced that with communist ideology. Since the collapse of the USSR, Russians haven't had a strong system of beliefs to call their own. Complicating matters is the fact that an estimated 20 to 30 million ethnic Russians live outside of their home country, mostly in Ukraine, Kazakhstan, and other former Soviet states. What is the real Russia, and who are the real Russians? No one knows the answer.

Russia is a fractured nation that doesn't quite know how to pull itself back together. "No new morality and ideology, which could have been a foundation for building a competitive new Russia, has emerged," wrote a group of young people with the Valdai Discussion

Can Russia gather its people together to move ahead? Will the economy diversify enough? And what are Putin's plans for the future? The children wait and dance.

Club in a 2014 paper titled "National Identity and the Future of Russia." The paper attempts to define an identity and envision a path towards a brighter future for Russia.

However, the Russia of tomorrow will be defined not by its past, but by the young people of today—people like Victoria. The way that Russians choose to see themselves and their homeland will change the direction of the country's future, either towards authoritarianism and isolationism, or towards openness, tolerance, and innovation. *

Russia in the news

RUSSIA

Text-Dependent Questions

1. What kind of society does communist ideology describe? How was actual communism in Russia different?
2. What would you expect to happen if you visited a Russian family in its home?
3. What industry is most important to Russia's economy, and why?
4. What happens during New Year's celebrations in Russia?
5. What does the Russian government do that takes away individual freedom?

Research Projects

1. Choose a Russian holiday. Look up traditional foods and activities that take place on this day, and write a story about a family celebrating the holiday. As extra credit, find a recipe for one of the traditional foods and prepare it at home.

2. Listen to a piece of music written by a Russian composer, such as Tchaikovsky, Rachmaninoff, or Shostakovich. Then read about the composer's life. Afterwards, listen to the music again. How have your feelings about the music changed?

3. Read about the conflict in the Ukraine and make a timeline of significant events. What do you think will happen between Ukraine and Russia in the future?

RUSSIA

Find Out More

Books

Haugen, David and Susan Musser, ed. *Opposing Viewpoints: Russia*. Farmington Hills, MI: Greenhaven Press, 2014.

Pavlovskaya, Anna. *CultureShock! Russia: A Survival Guide to Customs and Etiquette*. New York: Marshall Cavendish Corporation, 2007.

Stein, Richard Joseph, ed. *Russia*. New York: H.W. Wilson Co., 2010.

Websites

rbth.com/
Russia Beyond the Headlines is a website with news, opinions, and more relating to politics, culture, business, science, and public life in Russia.

www.russia-direct.org/
Russia Direct publishes articles that focus on Russia's relationship with the United States and other countries in the world.

masterrussian.com/
Though this website focuses on teaching the Russian language, it also includes information on culture and customs.

www.cia.gov/Library/publications/the-world-factbook/geos/rs.html
Learn factual information about Russia, including its geography, economic statistics, population statistics, and more.

Series Glossary of Key Terms

arable land   land suitable for cultivation and the growing of crops

commodity   a raw material that has value and is regularly bought and sold

cuisine   cooking that is characteristic of a particular country, region, or restaurant

destabilize   damage, disrupt, undermine

dynasties   long periods of time during which one extended family rules a place

industrialization   the process in which an economy is transformed from mainly agricultural to one based on manufacturing goods

infrastructure   buildings, roads, services, and other things that are necessary for a society to function

lunar calendar   a calendar based on the period from one moon to the next. Each cycle is 28 1/2 to 29 days, so the lunar year is about 354 days

parliamentary   describes a government in which a body of cabinet ministers is chosen from the legislature and act as advisers to the chief of state (or prime minister)

resonate   echo and reverberate; stay current through time

sovereignty   having supreme power and authority

venerate   treat with great respect

RUSSIA

INDEX

art, 22, 25-27
ballet, 22, 26
censorship, 27, 56
churches, 25-26
climate, 10-11
Cold War, 14-15
collectivism, 15
communism, 13-15, 44
dissidents, 54, 57
drinks, 22, 24-25
economic turmoil, 44
economy, 46-48, 50, 55
education, 18-19
entertainment, 22, 43
exports, 46-47
family celebrations, 36-38
food, 20-24
fragmentation, 55, 58-59
funerals, 39
geography, 11
government, 44, 48-50, 56

history, 12-17
holidays, 32-35
hospitality, 22-23, 25
income inequality, 45
labor market, 48
language, 29
Lenin, Vladimir, 12-14
literature, 22, 26-27
manufacturing, 47
Marxism, 13
Moscow, 9, 11, 31, 38, 45
music, 22, 26, 50
national identity, 16-17, 58-59
natural gas, 46-47
oil, 46-47, 55
oligarchs, 44
Olympic Games, 28-29
population, 44-45
prime ministers, 15
propaganda, 27
Putin, Vladimir, 15-16, 44, 48-

50, 54, 57-58
religion, 32-33
religious icons, 25-26
revolutions, 12
Russian Orthodox Church, 32
sanctions, 50
scientists, 27-28
secular holidays, 32, 35-36
social customs, 40-41
Soviet Union, 32, 44, 49
sports, 22, 27-29
St. Petersburg, 9, 11, 30
superstitions, 32, 41
terrain, 11
Trump, Donald, President, 58
tsars, 12
Union of Soviet Socialist
  Republics, 13-15
weddings, 37-38
World War II, 14

Photo Credits

Adobe Images: Peter Hermes Furian 11, ffphoto 20, Markus Mainka 20, Marcelokrelling 20, OlegD 21, Olena Danileiko 21 (2), hiphoto39 23, RNG 24, Elisheva Monasevich 25, Dimbar76 35, mastrovideo 38, olezzo 40. AP Images: SIPA 55. Dreamstime.com: Andrey Anisimov 9t, Xantana 9b, Joachim Eckel 16, Photographerlondon 18, Kostyantin Pankin 19, Igor Golovniov 19, Bozhdb 19, Lobur 21, Jackq 26, Viovita 28, Alexirina27000 30r, Nikolaev 30l, Olena Buyskykh 31, Catuncia 33, Igor Dolgov 36, Ryzhov Sergey 37, Fotoska 39, Jarenwicklund 42, cylon photo 43, Alenmax 45, George Spade 46, DyMax 51, Boris Akhunov 53, Evgeny Prokofyev 53, Alexey Kuznetsov 53, Yurataranik 52, Pavel Losevksky 57, Foryouinf 59. Google Art Project: 27. Newscom: Matthew Schofield/TNS 49, Tatyana Makeyeva 56. Wikiwand: 12, Ephraim Stillberg 14.

Author Bio

Kathryn Hulick served in the Peace Corps in Kyrgyzstan, a former Soviet republic, for two years. There, she became familiar with the Russian language, customs, food, and culture. She celebrated New Year's, International Women's Day, and Victory Day, and ate lots of *pelmeni*. She now lives in Massachusetts with her husband and son. They like to hike, read, cook, visit the ocean, and play with their dog, Maya. Hulick has written numerous books and articles for children and young adults, about everything from outer space to video games. ("Spasibo!" to Dr. David Ginsberg for his help in connecting with Victoria and her family.)